PHOTOCOPIABLE Mental Arithmetic Questions Book 4

by Helen Maden

Mental Arithmetic Questions Book 4 is one of a series of four books which provide a bank of easily accessible Mental Arithmetic Questions for use in a variety of classroom situations. It contains thirty different exercises which progressively get harder. Each exercise includes: Teacher Questions suitable for reading aloud, all answers needed and a photocopiable Pupil Answer Sheet with prompts given where necessary.

Book 4 includes work from The National Curriculum Levels 3, 4 and 5, mathematical problems using numbers up to 1,000,000 and concepts taken from The National Numeracy Strategy Key Objectives for Year Six.

Topical Resources publishes a range of Educational Materials for use in Primary Schools and Pre-School Nurseries and Playgroups.

For latest catalogue:
Tel: 01772 863158
Fax: 01772 866153

E.Mail: sales@topical-resources.co.uk
Visit our Website on:
www.topical-resources.co.uk

Copyright © 1999 Helen Maden
Illustrated by Paul Sealey

Printed in Great Britain for "Topical Resources", Publishers of Educational Materials, P.O. Box 329, Broughton, Preston, PR3 5LT by T.Snape & Company Ltd, Boltons Court, Preston, England.

Typeset by Paul Sealey Illustration and Design, 3 Wentworth Drive, Thornton, England. FY5 5AR.

First Published September 1999.
ISBN 1 872977 47 2

Contents

Test 1 . . . .
Test 2 . . . .
Test 3 . . . . Page 8
Test 4 . . . . Page 10
Test 5 . . . . Page 12
Test 6 . . . . Page 14
Test 7 . . . . Page 16
Test 8 . . . . Page 18
Test 9 . . . . Page 20
Test 10 . . . . Page 22
Test 11 . . . . Page 24
Test 12 . . . . Page 26
Test 13 . . . . Page 28
Test 14 . . . . Page 30
Test 15 . . . . Page 32
Test 16 . . . . Page 34
Test 17 . . . . Page 36
Test 18 . . . . Page 38
Test 19 . . . . Page 40
Test 20 . . . . Page 42
Test 21 . . . . Page 44
Test 22 . . . . Page 46
Test 23 . . . . Page 48
Test 24 . . . . Page 50
Test 25 . . . . Page 52
Test 26 . . . . Page 54
Test 27 . . . . Page 56
Test 28 . . . . Page 58
Test 29 . . . . Page 60
Test 30 . . . . Page 62

Teacher's Notes

How the Books are Organised
This book is one of a series of four. It contains thirty Mental Arithmetic exercises which use a wide mathematical vocabulary as advocated in The National Numeracy Strategy. Each exercise consists of a page of Teacher Questions together with answers and a photocopiable Pupil Answer Sheet complete with all necessary prompts. The book also includes a master for a Teacher's Record Sheet and a Pupil Record Sheet.

Each exercise has been designed to begin with three easier questions so that every child in the group will be able to achieve some positive results.

Repetitive questions allow the children to become familiar with a large variety of problems. To make the activities suitably taxing, the questions progress from easy at the beginning of the book to harder ones towards the end.

Book 1 includes work from The National Curriculum Levels 2 and 3, mathematical problems using numbers up to 500 and concepts taken from The National Numeracy Strategy Key Objectives for Year Three.

Book 2 includes work from The National Curriculum Levels 2, 3 and 4, mathematical problems using numbers up to 1,000 and concepts taken from The National Numeracy Strategy Key Objectives for Year Four.

Book 3 includes work from The National Curriculum Levels 3 and 4, mathematical problems using numbers up to 10,000 and concepts taken from The National Numeracy Strategy Key Objectives for Year Five.

Book 4 includes work from The National Curriculum Levels 3, 4 and 5, mathematical problems using numbers up to 1,000,000 and concepts taken from The National Numeracy Strategy Key Objectives for Year Six.

How to Use the Questions
The questions in this book could be used in a number of different ways including:

(1) As the basis of quick fire mental oral work to be used at the introduction of a mathematics lesson.

(2) As a Diagnostic Test to assess understanding and ability to solve Mental Arithmetic questions.

(3) As preparation for end of year SATs tests.

The exercises in this book may be used to suggest questions for use in the quick fire oral mental session found at the beginning of every numeracy lesson. One approach could be to teach and practice questions of a similar type to those found on the exercise chosen for that week and then use the exercise as an assessment test at the end of the week.

Using the exercises as a diagnostic aid would involve carrying out a test with the children, then tomark the work, identify common misconceptions and use this information to inform planning and subsequent teaching. The children could then be re-tested at a later date to assess improvements made.

If the exercises are to be used to prepare children for annual SAT tests, the teacher would read each question aloud twice and then count silently five, ten or fifteen seconds (depending upon the time indicated in the teacher questions) before proceeding to the next question. Alternatively, the teacher may prefer to have a stop clock on his/her desk to help judge accurately the length of time given to help solve each problem.

At all times children should be discouraged from using any aids such as scrap paper, calculators, rulers, mirrors, protractors etc.and positively encouraged to as often as possible complete numerical operations in their heads!

The Teacher's Record Sheet
A teacher's record sheet is provided in order to keep track of the progress of each individual child. Spaces are provided to record the score obtained on each test. This can be used to identify pupils who need extra support, or more challenging material.

The Pupil's Record Sheet
A pupil record sheet is provided which can be photocopied for each child. A simple way for them to record their results in each test would be to shade along each row up to the mark obtained on that occasion. These results could be then read as a real life bar chart.

Teacher's Record Sheet

Class _____ Date Started _____

Pupil's Name	Test 1	Test 2	Test 3	Test 4	Test 5	Test 6	Test 7	Test 8	Test 9	Test 10	Test 11	Test 12	Test 13	Test 14	Test 15	Test 16	Test 17	Test 18	Test 19	Test 20	Test 21	Test 22	Test 23	Test 24	Test 25	Test 26	Test 27	Test 28	Test 29	Test 30

© **Topical Resources.** May be photocopied for classroom use only.

Book 4 Test 1 Teacher Questions

No.	Question	Answer
	Five Second Questions	
1	How much do three twenty pence stamps cost?	60p
2	What is ten more than sixty seven?	77
3	What is the total of three hundred, twenty and six?	326
4	Add together seven, three and twenty four.	34
5	Change five and a half metres into centimetres.	550cm
6	What is twenty seven divided by nine?	3
7	Write one even number which is more than ten and less than twenty.	12,14,16,18
8	Four people share one pound equally. How much do they get each?	25p
	Ten Second Questions	
9	On your answer sheet, what is the number shown by the arrow.	4.7
10	What number is sixteen less than one hundred and six?	90
11	Multiply two by ten and then add one.	21
12	How many seconds are there in six minutes?	360 seconds
13	What is the size of this angle.	25° - 35°
14	Divide twenty by four then add six.	11
15	146 is added to a number. The answer is 497. What is the number?	351
	Fifteen Second Questions	
16	In a game there are 3 blue balls and 7 green balls. What is the chance of picking a green ball?	7/10
17	If a playing field is 26m wide by 76m long. what is the perimeter?	204m
18	If the ratio of boys to girls is 3:1 and there are 4 girls, how many boys are there?	12 boys
19	What is the mode of these six numbers: 7, 4, 6, 7, 5, 3 ?	7
20	What are the coordinates of the point marked on the sheet?	(3, 2)

Book 4 Test 1 Pupil Answer Sheet

Name_____   Date_____   Total Score ☐

Five Second Questions

1. _____ p
2. _____
3. _____
4. _____
5. _____ cm
6. _____
7. _____
8. _____ p

Ten Second Questions

9. _____   (ruler diagram: 4 to 5 with arrow)
10. _____

11. _____
12. _____ seconds
13. _____ degrees   (angle diagram)
14. _____
15. _____   146 , 497

Fifteen Second Questions

16. _____   3 blue balls / 7 green balls
17. _____ m   26m , 76m
18. _____ boys   3:1 , 4 girls
19. _____   7, 4, 6, 7, 5, 3
20. _____   (coordinate grid with x marked at (3,2))

© Topical Resources. May be photocopied for classroom use only.

5

Book 4 Test 2 Teacher Questions

No.	Question	Answer
	Five Second Questions	
1	What is the total of fifteen and fifteen?	30
2	There are 14 boys and 12 girls in a class. How many children altogether?	26 children
3	What is the nearest ten to sixty nine?	70
4	What is four point six multiplied by one hundred?	460
5	What is two hundred and forty six to the nearest hundred?	200
6	In a survey one half of the people liked singing. What percentage is this?	50%
7	What is double thirty five?	70
8	What is one quarter of forty?	10
	Ten Second Questions	
9	A T.V. show starts at 6 o'clock. It lasts for 35 minutes. When does it finish?	6:35
10	If one book costs £2.99, how much will six books cost?	£17.94
11	What is fifteen percent of sixty?	9
12	What is half of two point six?	1.3
13	A shop has a half price sale. A book was £19. How much is it now?	£9.50
14	In London the temperature is -6°C. In Madrid it is 16°C. What is the difference?	22°C
15	Circle the two numbers that total forty six.	12 & 34
	Fifteen Second Questions	
16	What is the mean of : 6, 9, 8, 10 and 7?	8
17	Look at the table on your sheet. How long does it take to get from the Town Centre to the Country Park?	30 minutes
18	What is the median of these seven numbers: 7, 8, 6, 4, 2, 9 & 17 ?	7
19	Subtract the sum of eight and nine from sixty three.	46
20	Put a circle round two numbers which are multiples of eight.	16 & 24

Book 4 Test 2 Pupil Answer Sheet

Name_____ Date_____ Total Score ☐

Five Second Questions

1. ☐
2. ☐ children
3. ☐
4. ☐
5. ☐
6. ☐ %
7. ☐
8. ☐

Ten Second Questions

9. ☐ 6:00 , 35 mins
10. £ ☐ £2.99 , 6
11. ☐ 15% , 60
12. ☐ 2.6
13. £ ☐ £19
14. ☐ °C London -6°C Madrid 16°C
15. ☐ 12   19   34   14   18

Fifteen Second Questions

16. ☐ 6, 9, 8, 10, 7

17. ☐ minutes

Bus Timetable	
Bus Station	9:00
Town Centre	9:10
Railway Station	9:16
Cinema	9:25
Country Park	9:40

18. ☐ 7, 8, 6, 4, 2, 9, 17
19. ☐ 8, 9, 63
20. ☐ 16   14   24   21   18   26

© Topical Resources. May be photocopied for classroom use only.

7

Book 4 Test 3 Teacher Questions

No.	Question	Answer
	Five Second Questions	
1	Write the next odd number after twenty five.	27
2	How much do six ten pence stamps cost?	60p
3	What is sixty take away twenty?	40
4	Write the number which is four less than two thousand.	1996
5	What is seven multiplied by eight?	56
6	Five people share 100 sweets equally. How many does each one get?	20 sweets
7	What is sixteen times one thousand?	16000
8	What is fifty percent of seventy?	35
	Ten Second Questions	
9	Jane paid for a jumper with a twenty pound note and got one penny change. How much did the jumper cost?	£19.99
10	What is two quarters in its simplest form?	$^1/_2$
11	What is the size of the angle printed on your sheet.	75° - 85°
12	Ten percent of a number is seventeen. What is the number?	170
13	If one sixth of a number is five, what is the number?	30
14	Sarah collects 10p coins. She has £11. How many coins does she have?	110 coins
15	Multiply seven hundred by sixty.	42000
	Fifteen Second Questions	
16	What is half of eight point two?	4.1
17	If a swimming pool measures 25m by 10m, what is its surface area?	250m^2
18	Look at the two numbers on your sheet. What number is half way between?	30
19	Put a circle around the two numbers which are factors of sixteen.	4 & 2
20	If Ashley saves 50p a week and needs £3.75 to buy a game, how many weeks will it be before he can buy it?	8 weeks

Book 4 Test 3 Pupil Answer Sheet

Name_____ Date_____ Total Score ☐

Five Second Questions

1. _____
2. _____ p
3. _____
4. _____
5. _____
6. _____ sweets
7. _____
8. _____

Ten Second Questions

9. £ _____   £20 , 1p
10. _____

11. _____ degrees
12. _____
13. _____
14. _____ coins   10p , £11
15. _____   700 , 60

Fifteen Second Questions

16. _____
17. _____ m²   25m , 10m
18. _____   27 , 33
19. _____   4 7 2 9 5 6
20. _____ weeks   50p , £3.75

© Topical Resources. May be photocopied for classroom use only.

9

Book 4 Test 4 Teacher Questions

No.	Question	Answer
	Five Second Questions	
1	What is the total of two hundred, fifty and six?	256
2	What is half of twelve?	6
3	What is ten more than sixty nine?	79
4	Write the number twenty thousand and six in figures.	20,006
5	What is the number which is one hundred and one before six hundred?	499
6	What is three hundred and seven to the nearest ten?	310
7	Subtract nine from seventeen.	8
8	Write an odd number which is more than fifteen and less than twenty.	17 or 19
	Ten Second Questions	
9	How many seconds are there in seven minutes?	420 seconds
10	What is the number shown by the arrow on your answer sheet.	8.3
11	Write four tenths as a decimal.	0.4
12	Multiply ten by three and then add nine.	39
13	What is minus six added to seven?	1
14	One seventh of a number is seven. What is the number?	49
15	Multiply six hundred by forty.	24000
	Fifteen Second Questions	
16	Look at the table on your sheet. How many dinners are served in a week?	45 dinners
17	Put these numbers in order, smallest first. 1.21, 1.194 and 1.7	1.194, 1.21, 1.7
18	In a game there are 7 yellow balls and 4 red balls. What is the chance of picking a red ball?	4/11
19	What year is it 300 years after 2004?	2304
20	What are the coordinates of the point marked on your sheet?	(4,1)

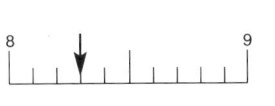

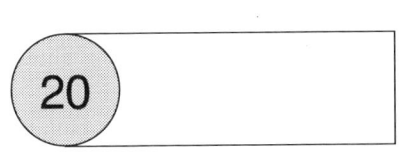

Book 4 Test 4 Pupil Answer Sheet

Name_____ Date_____ Total Score ☐

Five Second Questions

1. ⬜
2. ⬜
3. ⬜
4. ⬜
5. ⬜   101 , 600
6. ⬜
7. ⬜
8. ⬜

Ten Second Questions

9. ⬜ seconds
10. ⬜   8 ↓ 9

11. ⬜
12. ⬜
13. ⬜
14. ⬜
15. ⬜   600 , 40

Fifteen Second Questions

Children Having School Dinners	
Monday	7
Tuesday	9
Wednesday	4
Thursday	8
Friday	17

16. ⬜ dinners
17. ⬜   1.21 , 1.194 , 1.7
18. ⬜   7 yellow balls
         4 red balls
19. ⬜   2004
20. ⬜

© **Topical Resources.** May be photocopied for classroom use only.

Book 4 Test 5 Teacher Questions

No.	Question	Answer
	Five Second Questions	
1	What is the total of twenty five and twenty five?	50
2	There are 15 boys and 15 girls in a class. How many children altogether?	30 children
3	What is the nearest ten to forty three?	40
4	Add together two, eight and sixteen.	26
5	What is double forty two?	84
6	Change four and a half metres into centimetres.	450cm
7	What is fifty four divided by nine?	6
8	Eight people share £4 equally. How much do they get each?	50p
	Ten Second Questions	
9	What is half of four point two?	2.1
10	What is fifteen percent of eighty?	12
11	A quarter of a number is seven. What is the number?	28
12	In Moscow the temperature is -4°C. In Majorca it is 20°C. What is the difference?	24°C
13	Divide sixteen by four and then add two.	6
14	What number is twenty eight less than one hundred and eight?	80
15	When 125 is added to a number the answer is 367. What is the number?	242
	Fifteen Second Questions	
16	Look at the graph on your sheet. How far will I have walked after 20 minutes?	2Km
17	A playing field measures 41m by 80m. What is the perimeter?	242m
18	What is the mode of these six numbers: 8, 8, 2, 4, 7, & 8?	8
19	If the ratio of boys to girls is 5:1 and there are 5 girls, how many boys are there?	25 boys
20	Subtract the sum of seventeen and eighteen from ninety two.	57

Book 4 Test 5 Pupil Answer Sheet

Name_____ Date_____ Total Score ☐

Five Second Questions

1. ⬭ _____
2. ⬭ _____ children
3. ⬭ _____
4. ⬭ _____
5. ⬭ _____
6. ⬭ _____ cm
7. ⬭ _____
8. ⬭ _____ p

Ten Second Questions

9. ⬭ _____   4.2
10. ⬭ _____   15% , 80

11. ⬭ _____
12. ⬭ _____ °C   Moscow -4°C
                        Majorca 20°C
13. ⬭ _____
14. ⬭ _____
15. ⬭ _____   125 , 367

Fifteen Second Questions

My Journey to School (graph)

16. ⬭ _____ km
17. ⬭ _____ m   41m , 80m
18. ⬭ _____   8, 8, 2, 4, 7, 8
19. ⬭ _____ boys 5:1 , 5 girls
20. ⬭ _____   17 , 18 , 92

© Topical Resources. May be photocopied for classroom use only.

13

Book 4 Test 6 Teacher Questions

No.	Question	Answer
	Five Second Questions	
1	What is ninety take away thirty?	60
2	How much do seven ten pence stamps cost?	70p
3	Write the next even number after thirty.	32
4	How many nines make ninety?	10
5	What is two point six multiplied by ten?	26
6	What are six lots of seven?	42
7	In a survey 1/4 of the people liked watching the weather forecast. What percentage liked watching the weather forecast?	25%
8	What is one quarter of twenty four?	6
	Ten Second Questions	
9	Simon paid for a tape with a £5 note and received 5p change. How much was the tape?	£4.95
10	A T.V. programme starts at 20 to 7. It lasts for 25mins. When does it finish?	7:05
11	A shop has a 1/2 price sale. A jumper was £31. How much does it cost now?	£15.50
12	If strawberries cost £2.99 a pack, how much will eight packs cost?	£23.92
13	What is the size of this angle.	40° - 50°
14	Tom collects 10p coins. He has £20. How many 10p coins does he have?	200 coins
15	Circle the two numbers that total twenty six.	12 & 14
	Fifteen Second Questions	
16	What is the mean of 4, 7, 6, 10 and 8?	7
17	What is half of 6.4?	3.2
18	What number comes exactly half way between the two numbers on your sheet?	4.4
19	What is the median of these seven numbers: 4, 2, 9, 18, 26, 7 and 3?	7
20	Circle two numbers which are multiples of seven.	21 & 49

Book 4 Test 6 Pupil Answer Sheet

Name_____   Date_____   Total Score ☐

Five Second Questions

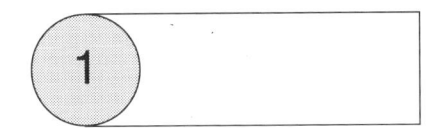

1) _____

2) _____ p

3) _____

4) _____

5) _____

6) _____

7) _____ %

8) _____

Ten Second Questions

9) £ _____   £5 , 5p

10) _____

11) £ _____

12) £ _____   £2.99 , 8

13) _____ degrees

14) _____ coins   10p , £20

15) _____   13 , 12 , 16 , 14 , 18

Fifteen Second Questions

16) _____   4, 7, 6, 10, 8

17) _____

18) _____   4.2 , 4.6

19) _____   4, 2, 9, 18, 26, 7, 3

20) _____   17 47 21 49 72 76

© Topical Resources. May be photocopied for classroom use only.

15

Book 4 Test 7 Teacher Questions

No.	Question	Answer
	Five Second Questions	
1	What is ten more than nineteen?	29
2	What is the nearest ten to forty six?	50
3	What is the total of seven hundred, sixty and three?	763
4	What is fifty percent of twenty two?	11
5	Write the number that is six less than five hundred.	494
6	Four people share twenty four sweets equally. How many do they get each?	6 sweets
7	What is twenty eight times one thousand?	28,000
8	What is six squared?	36
	Ten Second Questions	
9	How many seconds in three and a half minutes?	210 seconds
10	Multiply two by six and then add seven.	19
11	What is two sixths in its simplest form?	1/3
12	Ten percent of a number is fourteen. What is the number?	140
13	Write five tenths as a decimal.	0.5
14	What is the square root of 81 added to 46?	55
15	One eighth of a number is eight. What is the number?	64
	Fifteen Second Questions	
16	On your sheet, circle two numbers which are factors of thirty two.	16 & 4
17	Look at the table on your sheet. How many dinners are served in a week?	37 dinners
18	A swimming pool measures 27m by 10m. What is its surface area?	270 m^2
19	If Sarah saves 50p per week and needs £4.25 to buy a book, how many weeks will it be before she can buy it?	9 weeks
20	What are the coordinates of the point marked on your sheet?	(-2, 2)

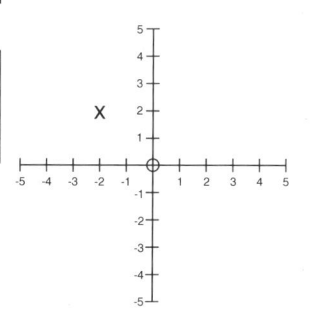

Book 4 Test 7 Pupil Answer Sheet

Name_____ Date_____ Total Score ☐

Five Second Questions

1. ☐
2. ☐
3. ☐
4. ☐
5. ☐
6. ☐ sweets
7. ☐
8. ☐

Ten Second Questions

9. ☐ seconds
10. ☐

11. ☐ $^2/_6$
12. ☐
13. ☐
14. ☐
15. ☐

Fifteen Second Questions

16. ☐ 16 7 4 12 9 5
17. ☐ dinners

Children Having School Dinners	
Monday	7
Tuesday	8
Wednesday	4
Thursday	8
Friday	10

18. ☐ m^2 27m , 10m
19. ☐ weeks 50p , £4.25
20. ☐

© **Topical Resources.** May be photocopied for classroom use only.

17

Book 4 Test 8 Teacher Questions

No.	Question	Answer
	Five Second Questions	
1	There are 17 girls and 12 boys in a class. How many children are there altogether?	29 children
2	What is half of fourteen?	7
3	What is the total of twenty two and twenty two?	44
4	Add together three, nine and twelve.	24
5	Write the number forty thousand and twenty three in figures.	40,023
6	Round off twenty nine to the nearest ten.	30
7	Write an even number more than twenty four and less than twenty eight.	26
8	Subtract eleven from twenty seven.	16
	Ten Second Questions	
9	In Moscow the temperature is -7°C. In Athens it is 14°C. What is the difference?	21°C
10	What is fifteen percent of forty?	6
11	What is the number shown by the arrow on your sheet.	12.2
12	Multiply forty by seven hundred.	28,000
13	Liz collects 20p coins. She has £16. How many 20p coins does she have?	80 x 20p coins
14	What is half of six point eight?	3.4
15	One tenth of a number is seventeen. What is the number?	170
	Fifteen Second Questions	
16	Look at the pie chart. What is the fraction of children who prefer Art.	1/4
17	Subtract the sum of sixteen and fifteen from eighty seven.	56
18	If the ratio of boys to girls is 5:1, and there are 10 boys, how many girls ?	2 girls
19	What year is two hundred years after two thousand and seven?	2207
20	What is the product of twenty five and twelve?	300

Book 4 Test 8 Pupil Answer Sheet

Name_____   Date_____   Total Score ☐

Five Second Questions

1. _____ children
2. _____
3. _____
4. _____
5. _____
6. _____
7. _____
8. _____

Ten Second Questions

9. _____ °C   Moscow -7°C
                    Athens 14°C
10. _____   15% , 40

11. _____   12 ↓ 13
12. _____   40 , 700
13. _____ 20p coins   20p , £16
14. _____   6.8
15. _____

Fifteen Second Questions

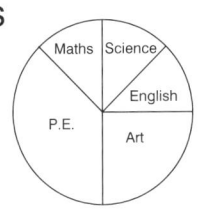

16. _____
17. _____   16 , 15 , 87
18. _____ girls   5:1 , 10 boys
19. _____   2007
20. _____   25 , 12

Book 4 Test 9 Teacher Questions

No.	Question	Answer
	Five Second Questions	
1	Write the next odd number after twenty seven.	29
2	How much do four five pence stamps cost?	20p
3	What is forty take away twenty?	20
4	What is seventy two divided by nine?	8
5	Five people share thirty five pence equally. How much do they get each?	7p
6	What is seven point four multiplied by ten?	74
7	Change ten metres into centimetres.	1000cm
8	What is ten percent of ninety?	9
	Ten Second Questions	
9	Divide twenty four by six and then add nine.	13
10	Rachel gave £10 for a CD. She got £1.01 change. How much was the CD?	£8.99
11	What is the size of this angle.	105° - 115°
12	What number is twenty four less than one hundred and four?	80
13	A shop has a half price sale. A chair was £43. How much is it now?	£21.50
14	If tapes cost three pounds ninety nine, how much will seven tapes cost?	£27.93
15	One quarter of a number is ten. What is the number?	40
	Fifteen Second Questions	
16	In a game there are 4 blue and 10 yellow balls. What is the chance of picking a yellow ball?	10/14 or 5/7
17	Put these numbers in order, largest first. 4.29, 4.672, and 4.17	4.672, 4.29, 4.17
18	What is the mean of 10, 20, 30, 40 and 50?	30
19	What is the mode of these six numbers: 8, 4, 9, 1, 2 and 1?	1
20	A playing field measures 29m by 41m. What is the perimeter of the field?	140m

Book 4 Test 9 Pupil Answer Sheet

Name_____ Date_____ Total Score ☐

Five Second Questions

1. _____
2. _____ p
3. _____
4. _____
5. _____ p
6. _____
7. _____ cm
8. _____

Ten Second Questions

9. _____
10. £ _____   £10 , £1.01

11. _____ degrees
12. _____
13. £ _____
14. £ _____   £3.99 , 7
15. _____

Fifteen Second Questions

16. _____   4 blue balls
                10 yellow balls
17. _____   4.29, 4.672, 4.17
18. _____   10, 20, 30, 40, 50
19. _____   8, 4, 9, 1, 2, 1
20. _____ m   29m , 41m

© **Topical Resources.** May be photocopied for classroom use only.

21

Book 4 Test 10 Teacher Questions

No.	Question	Answer
	Five Second Questions	
1	What is the nearest ten to sixty five?	70
2	What is ten more than sixty three?	73
3	What is the total of six hundred, two and thirty?	632
4	What is double twenty three?	46
5	What is six hundred and seventy two to the nearest hundred?	700
6	In a survey three quarters of the people had pets. What percentage had pets?	75%
7	What is six multiplied by eight?	48
8	What is a quarter of sixteen?	4
	Ten Second Questions	
9	How many seconds in seven and a half minutes?	450 seconds
10	When 167 is added to a number the answer is 289. What is the number?	122
11	A TV programme starts at a quarter to eight. It finishes forty minutes later. At what time does it finish?	8:25
12	Multiply seven by eight and then add three.	59
13	In Glasgow the temperature is -2°C. In Palma it is 26°C. What is the difference?	28°C
14	Circle the two numbers that total seventy five.	60 & 15
15	Write one tenth as a decimal.	0.1
	Fifteen Second Questions	
16	What is the median of these seven numbers: 9, 2, 11, 22, 46, 21 and 7?	11
17	What is half of eight point six?	4.3
18	What number is exactly half way between the two numbers on your sheet?	79
19	Put a circle round the numbers which are multiples of six.	36 & 18
20	What are the coordinates of the point marked on your sheet?	(-4, 3)

Book 4 Test 10 Pupil Answer Sheet

Name_____ Date_____ Total Score ☐

Five Second Questions

1. ⬜
2. ⬜
3. ⬜
4. ⬜
5. ⬜
6. ⬜ %
7. ⬜
8. ⬜

Ten Second Questions

9. ⬜ seconds   7½ minutes
10. ⬜   167 , 289
11. ⬜   ¼ to 8 , 40mins
12. ⬜
13. ⬜ °C   Glasgow -2°C
              Palma 26°C
14. ⬜   16 60 20 15 17
15. ⬜

Fifteen Second Questions

16. ⬜   9, 2, 11, 22, 46, 21, 7
17. ⬜
18. ⬜   76 , 82
19. ⬜   36 18 17 46 22 26
20. ⬜

© **Topical Resources.** May be photocopied for classroom use only.

23

Book 4 Test 11 Teacher Questions

No.	Question	Answer
	Five Second Questions	
1	There are thirty children in a class. Three are absent. How many are present?	27 children
2	What is seventy take away twenty?	50
3	What is the total of thirty one and thirty one?	62
4	What is fifty percent of forty six?	23
5	What is forty six times one thousand?	46,000
6	Write the number that is four less than six hundred.	596
7	Write the number sixty one thousand and six in figures.	61,006
8	Five people share 150 sweets equally. How many do they get each?	30 sweets
	Ten Second Questions	
9	What is twenty-nine added to fourteen?	43
10	What is fifteen percent of one hundred and twenty?	18
11	Multiply ninety by six hundred.	54,000
12	What is the number shown by the arrow on your sheet.	20.9
13	What is the size of this angle.	5° - 15°
14	Ten percent of a number is twenty. What is the number?	200
15	What is five tenths in its simplest form?	one half
	Fifteen Second Questions	
16	Circle the three numbers which are factors of eighteen.	3 , 6 and 2
17	What year is four hundred years after two thousand and one?	2401
18	If the ratio of boys to girls is 7:2 and there are 4 girls, how many boys?	14 boys
19	Look at the timetable on your sheet. How long does it take to get from the town centre to the cinema?	15 minutes
20	A swimming pool is 30m by 20m. What is its surface area?	600 m²

Book 4 Test 11 Pupil Answer Sheet

Name_____ Date_____ Total Score ☐

Five Second Questions

1. _____ children
2. _____
3. _____
4. _____
5. _____
6. _____
7. _____
8. _____ sweets

Ten Second Questions

9. _____
10. _____ 15% , 120
11. _____ 90 , 600
12. _____
13. _____ degrees
14. _____
15. _____ 5/10

Fifteen Second Questions

16. _____ 2 3 4 7 6 5
17. _____ 2001
18. _____ boys   7:2 , 4 girls
19. _____ minutes

Bus Timetable	
Bus Station	9:00
Town Centre	9.10
Railway Station	9.16
Cinema	9.25
Country Park	9.40

20. _____ m² 30m , 20m

© **Topical Resources.** May be photocopied for classroom use only.

Book 4 Test 12 Teacher Questions

No.	Question	Answer
	Five Second Questions	
1	What is a quarter of twelve?	3
2	How much do two fifteen pence stamps cost?	30p
3	What is half of sixteen?	8
4	Add together four, seven and twenty four.	35
5	Write an odd number more than twenty and less than twenty five.	21 or 23
6	How many sevens make twenty one?	3
7	Subtract nine from thirty six.	27
8	What is five squared?	25
	Ten Second Questions	
9	Liam collects 20p coins. He has £12. How many 20p coins has he got?	60x20p coins
10	In Glasgow the temperature is -7°C. In Tenerife it is 24°C. What is the difference?	31°C
11	One sixth of a number is six. What is the number?	36
12	25% of a number is twenty. What is the number?	80
13	Multiply four hundred by two hundred.	80,000
14	What is half of nine point four?	4.7
15	Harry paid £5 for a T shirt. He got 75p change. How much was the T shirt?	£4.25
	Fifteen Second Questions	
16	If James saves £1.50 a week and needs £7.50 for a book, how many weeks will it be before he can buy it?	5 weeks
17	Subtract the sum of seven and eighteen from sixty four.	39
18	What is the number exactly half way between the numbers on your sheet?	94
19	Look at the table on your sheet. How many dinners are served in a week?	39 dinners
20	What is the product of twenty five and sixteen?	400

Book 4 Test 12 Pupil Answer Sheet

Name_____ Date_____ Total Score ☐

Five Second Questions

1. _____
2. _____ p
3. _____
4. _____
5. _____
6. _____
7. _____
8. _____

Ten Second Questions

9. _____ twenty pence coins   20p , £12
10. _____ °C   Glasgow -7°C   Tenerife 24°C

11. _____
12. _____
13. _____   400 , 200
14. _____   9.4
15. _____ £   £5 , 75p

Fifteen Second Questions

16. _____ weeks   £1.50 , £7.50
17. _____   7 , 18 , 64
18. _____   91 , 97
19. _____ dinners

Children Having School Dinners	
Monday	6
Tuesday	2
Wednesday	4
Thursday	8
Friday	19

20. _____   25 , 16

© Topical Resources. May be photocopied for classroom use only.

27

Book 4 Test 13 Teacher Questions

No.	Question	Answer
	Five Second Questions	
1	What is the total of nine hundred, forty and two?	942
2	Write the next even number after fifty.	52
3	What is ten more than seventy nine?	89
4	What is forty five divided by nine?	5
5	Change seven and a half metres into centimetres.	750cm
6	Six people share two pound forty equally. How much do they get each?	40p
7	What is three point two multiplied by ten?	32
8	Write the number ninety six thousand and seven.	96,007
	Ten Second Questions	
9	What number is twenty six less than one hundred and five?	79
10	Divide forty by ten and then add eleven.	15
11	How many minutes are there in seven hours?	420 minutes
12	A TV programme starts at a quarter past nine and lasts for fifty minutes. When does it finish?	10:05
13	A bag of potatoes costs £1.49. How many bags can you buy with £10?	6 bags
14	Multiply six by four and then subtract two.	22
15	One ninth of a number is four. What is the number?	36
	Fifteen Second Questions	
16	In a game there are six pink and four purple balls. What is the chance of picking a purple ball?	4/10 or 2/5
17	If each square is 1 cm^2, what is the area of the shape to the nearest 1/2 cm^2.	$5cm^2$ - $6cm^2$
18	A playing field measures 49m by 100m. What is the perimeter of the field?	298m
19	What is the mode of these five numbers: 7, 7, 4, 8 and 2?	7
20	What are the coordinates of the point marked on your sheet?	(3, -4)

Book 4 Test 13 Pupil Answer Sheet

Name_____ Date_____ Total Score ☐

Five Second Questions

1. ◯ _____
2. ◯ _____
3. ◯ _____
4. ◯ _____
5. ◯ _____ cm
6. ◯ _____ p
7. ◯ _____
8. ◯ _____

Ten Second Questions

9. ◯ _____   26 , 105
10. ◯ _____

11. ◯ _____ minutes
12. ◯ _____   ¼ past 9 , 50mins
13. ◯ _____ bags   £1.49 , £10
14. ◯ _____
15. ◯ _____

Fifteen Second Questions

16. ◯ _____   6 pink balls
     4 purple balls
17. ◯ _____ cm²
18. ◯ _____ m   49m , 100m
19. ◯ _____   7, 7, 4, 8, 2
20. ◯ _____

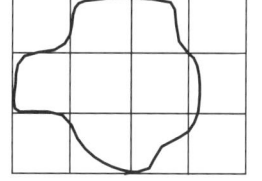

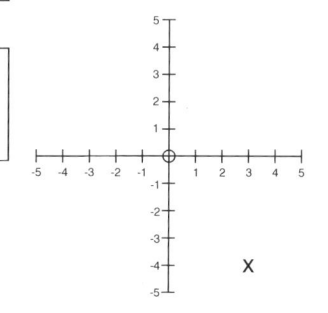

© **Topical Resources.** May be photocopied for classroom use only.

Book 4 Test 14 Teacher Questions

No.	Question	Answer
	Five Second Questions	
1	How much do three ten pence stamps cost?	30p
2	What is the nearest ten to ninety one?	90
3	There are thirty children in a class. Four are absent. How many are present?	26 children
4	What is one quarter of twenty?	5
5	Write the number one hundred and seventy thousand and twenty six in figures.	170,026
6	What is nine hundred and seven to the nearest ten?	910
7	What is four multiplied by eight?	32
8	What is double nineteen?	38
	Ten Second Questions	
9	If books cost £3.99 each, how much will eight books cost?	£31.92
10	What is the size of this angle.	$70°$ - $80°$
11	A shop has a half price sale. A jacket was £52. What is the price now?	£26
12	When 126 is added to a number the answer is 348. What is the number?	222
13	Write two tenths as a decimal.	0.2
14	Circle the two numbers that total eighty two.	40 & 42
15	Multiply ninety by seven hundred.	63,000
	Fifteen Second Questions	
16	What is the mean of 11, 12, and 16?	13
17	Put these numbers in order, smallest first. 8.91, 8.18 and 9.63	8.18, 8.91, 9.63
18	What is the median of these seven numbers: 9, 7, 4, 3, 5, 19 and 26?	7
19	A swimming pool measures 50m by 20m. What is its surface area?	1000 m^2
20	Look at the graph on your sheet. How far will I have walked after 40 minutes?	4 km

Book 4 Test 14 Pupil Answer Sheet

Name_____ Date_____ Total Score ☐

Five Second Questions

1) _____ p

2) _____

3) _____ children

4) _____

5) _____

6) _____

7) _____

8) _____

Ten Second Questions

9) £ _____   £3.99 , 8

10) _____ degrees

11) £ _____

12) _____   126 , 348

13) _____

14) _____   40 , 62 , 42 , 22 , 72

15) _____   90 , 700

Fifteen Second Questions

16) _____   11 , 12 , 16

17) _____   8.91, 8.18, 9.63

18) _____   9, 7, 4, 3, 5, 19, 26

19) _____ m²   50m , 20m

20) _____ km

My Journey to School

© Topical Resources. May be photocopied for classroom use only.

31

Book 4 Test 15 Teacher Questions

No.	Question	Answer
	Five Second Questions	
1	What is half of twenty two?	11
2	What is the total of six hundred, two and seventy?	672
3	What is eighty take away forty?	40
4	Add together nine, four and twelve.	25
5	Five people share thirty five sweets equally. How many do they get each?	7 sweets
6	Change seventy six metres into centimetres.	7600 cm
7	In a survey, 50% of the people asked liked riding a bike. What fraction of the people liked riding a bike?	a half
8	What is eight hundred and thirty divided by ten?	83
	Ten Second Questions	
9	Ten percent of a number is forty. What is the number?	400
10	What is fifteen percent of one hundred and sixty?	24
11	What is minus twelve add two?	-10
12	What is four tenths in its simplest form?	2/5
13	What is the number shown by the arrow on your sheet.	4.17
14	Divide eight thousand by forty.	200
15	I'm thinking of a number. I half it then add 4. The answer is 9. What is the number?	10
	Fifteen Second Questions	
16	What is half of seven point four plus 2.3?	6
17	Subtract the sum of fifteen and thirteen from forty six.	18
18	What year is seven hundred years after two thousand and nine?	2709
19	If the ratio of boys to girls is 5:2 and there are ten boys, how many girls?	4 girls
20	Circle the two numbers which are multiples of nine.	18 & 81

Book 4 Test 15 Pupil Answer Sheet

Name_____ Date_____ Total Score ☐

Five Second Questions

1.
2.
3.
4.
5.   sweets
6.   cm
7.
8.

Ten Second Questions

9.
10.   15% , 160

11.   -12 , 2
12.   ⁴/₁₀
13.   [scale 4.1 to 4.2 with arrow]
14.   8000 , 40
15.

Fifteen Second Questions

16.   7.4 , 2.3
17.   15 , 13 , 46
18.   2009
19.   girls   5:2 , 10 boys
20.   29 , 16 , 18 , 49 , 81 , 16

© Topical Resources. May be photocopied for classroom use only.

Book 4 Test 16 Teacher Questions

No.	Question	Answer
	Five Second Questions	
1	What is the total of twenty four and twenty one?	45
2	How much do three thirty pence stamps cost?	90p
3	Write the next odd number after seventeen.	19
4	Write an even number which is more than 100 and less than 105.	102 or 104
5	What is twenty five percent of forty?	10
6	Subtract eleven from forty eight.	37
7	Write the number that is twelve less than one hundred.	88
8	What is forty seven added to thirty?	77
	Ten Second Questions	
9	If a magazine costs £1.99, how many can you buy with £15?	7 magazines
10	Multiply seven by four and then add on six.	34
11	Jane collects 50p coins. She has £6.50. How many coins does she have?	13 x 50p coins
12	How many minutes are there in nine hours?	540 minutes
13	A quarter of a number is twenty five. What is the number?	100
14	In Paris the temperature is 24°C. In Moscow it is -7°C. What is the difference?	31°C
15	Twenty five percent of a number is sixteen. What is the number?	64
	Fifteen Second Questions	
16	What is the number exactly half way between the two numbers on your sheet?	89
17	Circle two numbers which are factors of twenty seven.	3 & 9
18	In a game there are six yellow and four white balls. What is the chance of picking a white ball?	4/10 or 2/5
19	A playing field measures 55m by 65m. What is the perimeter?	240 m
20	What are the coordinates of the point marked on your sheet	(0, -2)

Book 4 Test 16 Pupil Answer Sheet

Name_____   Date_____   Total Score ☐

Five Second Questions

1. _____
2. _____ p
3. _____
4. _____
5. _____
6. _____
7. _____
8. _____

Ten Second Questions

9. _____ magazines   £1.99 , £15
10. _____

11. _____ fifty pence coins   50p , £6.50
12. _____ minutes
13. _____
14. _____ °C   Paris 24°C   Moscow -7°C
15. _____

Fifteen Second Questions

16. _____   86 , 92
17. _____   3 , 4 , 6 , 9 , 7 , 6
18. _____   6 yellow balls   4 white balls
19. _____ m   55m , 65m
20. _____

© Topical Resources. May be photocopied for classroom use only.

35

Book 4 Test 17 Teacher Questions

No.	Question	Answer
	Five Second Questions	
1	What is ninety take away sixty?	30
2	There are 29 children in a class. Three are absent. How many are present?	26 children
3	What is half of eight?	4
4	What is fifty six divided by eight?	7
5	What is nine squared?	81
6	What is four multiplied by seven?	28
7	Five people shared two pound fifty equally. How much did they get each?	50p
8	What is seventeen point six multiplied by ten?	176
	Ten Second Questions	
9	Write nine tenths as a decimal.	0.9
10	What number is thirty four less than one hundred and fourteen?	80
11	One seventh of a number is six. What is the number?	42
12	What is the size of the angle on your sheet.	155° - 165°
13	A TV programme starts at twenty to seven. It lasts for forty five minutes. At what time does it finish?	7:25
14	Divide twenty eight by four and then add six.	13
15	If Chess Sets cost £6.99, how much will four chess sets cost?	£27.96
	Fifteen Second Questions	
16	Look at the pie chart on your sheet. What is the fraction of children who prefer Maths.	1/8
17	If Gill saves £1.50 a week and needs £9.50 to buy some new shoes, how many weeks will it be before she can afford them?	7 weeks
18	If a swimming pool is 30m by 12m, what is the surface area?	360 m^2
19	What is the mode of these six numbers: 2, 8, 4, 7, 8 and 6?	8
20	Look at the table on your sheet. How many dinners are served in a week?	33 dinners

Book 4 Test 17 Pupil Answer Sheet

Name_____   Date_____   Total Score ☐

Five Second Questions

1. ☐
2. ☐ children
3. ☐
4. ☐
5. ☐
6. ☐
7. ☐ p
8. ☐

Ten Second Questions

9. ☐
10. ☐

11. ☐
12. ☐ degrees
13. ☐ 20 to 7 , 45 mins
14. ☐
15. ☐ £   £6.99 , 4

Fifteen Second Questions

16. ☐

	Maths	Science	
P.E.		English	
		Art	

17. ☐ weeks   £1.50 , £9.50
18. ☐ m²   30m , 12m
19. ☐ 2, 8, 4, 7, 8, 6
20. ☐ dinners

Children Having School Dinners
Monday	3
Tuesday	7
Wednesday	0
Thursday	7
Friday	16

© Topical Resources. May be photocopied for classroom use only.

Book 4 Test 18 Teacher Questions

No.	Question	Answer
	Five Second Questions	
1	What is the nearest ten to sixty four?	60
2	What is ten more than forty seven?	57
3	What is the total of three hundred, forty and two?	342
4	What is the square root of one hundred?	10
5	What is double eighteen?	36
6	Write the number three hundred thousand and forty five in numerals.	300,045
7	What is four hundred and twelve to the nearest ten?	410
8	What is one quarter of eighty?	20
	Ten Second Questions	
9	Lisa paid for her trousers with a £10 note. Her change was 25p How much were the trousers?	£9.75
10	A shop has a half price sale. A table was £53. How much is it now?	£26.50
11	What is fifteen percent of eighty?	12
12	Ten percent of a number is nineteen. What is the number?	190
13	Divide five hundred and sixty by eighty.	7
14	What is half of seven point two?	3.6
15	What is the number shown by the arrow on your answer sheet.	8.44
	Fifteen Second Questions	
16	If each square measures 1 sq cm^2, what is the area of the shape to the nearest $1/2$ sq cm^2.	$5^{1}/_{2}$ - $6^{1}/_{2}$ cm^2
17	What is the mean of: 10, 12, 14, 20 and 24?	16
18	What is the median of these seven numbers: 18, 7, 6, 5, 7, 1 and 2?	6
19	What is half of five point eight, plus one point three?	4.2
20	What is the product of nine and twenty five?	225

Book 4 Test 18 Pupil Answer Sheet

Name_____ Date_____ Total Score

Five Second Questions

1.
2.
3.
4.
5.
6.
7.
8.

Ten Second Questions

9. £   £10 , 25p
10. £

11.   15% , 80
12.
13.   560 , 80
14.   7.2
15.   8.4   8.5

Fifteen Second Questions

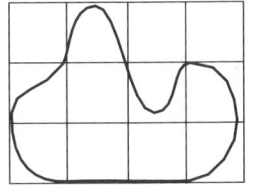

16.   cm²
17.   10, 12, 14, 20, 24
18.   18, 7, 6, 5, 7, 1, 2
19.   5.8 , 1.3
20.

© Topical Resources. May be photocopied for classroom use only.

39

Book 4 Test 19 Teacher Questions

No.	Question	Answer
	Five Second Questions	
1	Write the next odd number after thirty nine?	41
2	How much do five ten pence stamps cost?	50p
3	What is the total of twenty one and ten?	31
4	Add together three, five and twelve.	20
5	What is nine hundred and twenty times one hundred?	92,000
6	Six people share thirty sweets equally. How many do they get each?	5 sweets
7	In a survey 25% of people had a dog. What fraction of people had a dog?	1/4
8	Change one hundred and forty metres into centimetres.	14,000 cm
	Ten Second Questions	
9	James collects 50p coins. He has £18. How many coins does he have?	36 coins
10	One quarter of a number is twelve. What is the number?	48
11	Circle the two numbers that total seventy six.	43 & 33
12	What is minus ten added to twenty five?	15
13	When 112 is added to a number the answer is 376. What is the number?	264
14	How many minutes in five and a half hours?	330 minutes
15	What is twelve sixteenths in its simplest form?	3/4
	Fifteen Second Questions	
16	What are the coordinates of the point marked on your sheet?	(-2, -2)
17	What year is eight hundred years after two thousand and seven?	2807
18	Put these numbers in order, largest first. 8.321, 8.97, 8.871	8.97, 8.871, 8.321
19	If a swimming pool is 30m by 13m, what is its surface area?	390m^2
20	Circle the two numbers which are factors of twenty one.	3 & 7

Book 4 Test 19 Pupil Answer Sheet

Name_____ Date_____ Total Score

Five Second Questions

1. _____
2. _____ p
3. _____
4. _____
5. _____
6. _____ sweets
7. _____
8. _____ cm

Ten Second Questions

9. _____ fifty pence coins   50p , £18
10. _____

11. _____ 21 43 62 12 33
12. _____ -10 , 25
13. _____ 112 , 376
14. _____ minutes
15. _____ 12/16

Fifteen Second Questions

16. _____
17. _____ 2007
18. _____ 8.321, 8.97, 8.871
19. _____ m²   30m , 13m
20. _____ 8 9 3 6 4 7

© Topical Resources. May be photocopied for classroom use only.

41

Book 4 Test 20 Teacher Questions

No.	Question	Answer
	Five Second Questions	
1	There are 30 children in a class. Half are on a trip. How many are left?	15 children
2	What is forty take away thirty?	10
3	What is the nearest ten to forty eight?	50
4	Subtract thirteen from forty.	27
5	What is three multiplied by eight?	24
6	Write an odd number more than 130 and less than 135.	131 or 133
7	What is twenty five percent of twenty?	5
8	Write the number that is seventeen less than one hundred.	83
	Ten Second Questions	
9	If computer discs cost £8.99 a box, how much will 9 boxes cost?	£80.91
10	What number is thirty six less than one hundred and fourteen?	78
11	Twenty percent of a number is twenty five. What is the number?	125
12	Multiply six by five and then add seventeen.	47
13	What is the size of this angle.	$125°$ - $135°$
14	In Cape Town the temperature is $26°C$. In Aberdeen it is $-3°C$. What is the difference?	$29°C$
15	A box of chocolates costs £3.99. How many boxes can you buy with £10?	2 boxes
	Fifteen Second Questions	
16	If the ratio of boys to girls is 6:7 and there are 36 boys, how many girls are there?	42 girls
17	Look at the time table on your sheet. How long does it take to get from the railway station to the country park?	24 minutes
18	What is half of six point three plus one point nine?	5.05
19	Subtract the sum of twenty one and thirty nine from ninety two.	32
20	Circle two numbers which are multiples of eight.	24 & 56

Book 4 Test 20 Pupil Answer Sheet

Name_____ Date_____ Total Score ☐

Five Second Questions

1. _____ children
2. _____
3. _____
4. _____
5. _____
6. _____
7. _____
8. _____

Ten Second Questions

9. £ _____   £8.99 , 9
10. _____   36 , 114
11. _____
12. _____
13. _____ degrees
14. _____ °C   Cape Town 26°C   Aberdeen -3°C
15. _____ boxes   £3.99 , £10

Fifteen Second Questions

16. _____ girls   6:7 , 36 boys
17. _____ minutes

Bus Timetable	
Bus Station	9:00
Town Centre	9.10
Railway Station	9.16
Cinema	9.25
Country Park	9.40

18. _____   6.3 , 1.9
19. _____   21 , 39 , 92
20. _____   19 26 44 24 56 17

© Topical Resources. May be photocopied for classroom use only.

Book 4 Test 21 Teacher Questions

No.	Question	Answer
	Five Second Questions	
1	How many ten pence stamps can you buy with seventy pence?	7 x 10p stamps
2	What is the total of six, twenty and seven hundred?	726
3	What is ten more than eighty two?	92
4	What is four point four multiplied by ten?	44
5	What is eight squared?	64
6	What is eighty one divided by nine?	9
7	Six people share three pounds equally. How much do they get each?	50p
8	What is the difference between seventeen and twenty four?	7
	Ten Second Questions	
9	Divide four hundred by twenty.	20
10	What is fifteen percent of seventy?	10.5
11	What is the number shown by the arrow on your sheet?	12.69
12	A TV programme starts at 10 to 9 and lasts for 25mins. When does it finish?	9:15
13	Divide forty two by six and then add six.	13
14	Tom bought a tape with a £10 note. He had £2.50 change. How much was the tape?	£7.50
15	What is half of nine point four?	4.7
	Fifteen Second Questions	
16	What is the mode of these six numbers: 19, 43, 62, 43, 46 and 91?	43
17	In a game there are six brown and four black balls. What is the chance of picking a black ball?	4/10 or 2/5
18	What number comes exactly half way between the numbers on your sheet?	55
19	What is the mean of: 10, 20, 6, 4, 5 and 15?	10
20	Circle two factors of forty two.	6 & 7

Book 4 Test 21 Pupil Answer Sheet

Name_____   Date_____   Total Score ☐

Five Second Questions

1. _____ ten pence stamps
2. _____
3. _____
4. _____
5. _____
6. _____
7. _____ p
8. _____

Ten Second Questions

9. _____
10. _____ 15% , 70

11. _____ 12.6 ↓12.7
12. _____ 10 to 9 , 25 mins
13. _____
14. £ _____ £10 , £2.50
15. _____ 9.4

Fifteen Second Questions

16. _____ 19, 43, 62, 43, 46, 91
17. _____ 6 brown balls / 4 black balls
18. _____ 47 , 63
19. _____ 10, 20, 6, 4, 5, 15
20. _____ 6 , 10 , 7 , 12 , 20 , 19

© Topical Resources. May be photocopied for classroom use only.

Book 4 Test 22 Teacher Questions

No.	Question	Answer
	Five Second Questions	
1	What is the total of fifteen and fourteen?	29
2	There are 16 boys and 14 girls in a class. How many children altogether?	30 children
3	Write the next even number after forty eight.	50
4	What is one tenth of sixty?	6
5	What is the square root of twenty five?	5
6	What is double forty five?	90
7	What is seven hundred and seven to the nearest hundred?	700
8	Write the number nine hundred and one thousand and fifty two.	901,052
	Ten Second Questions	
9	A quarter of a number is twenty six. What is the number?	104
10	Sally collects 5p coins. She has £15. How many coins does she have?	300 coins
11	A shop has a half price sale. A picture was £71. How much is it now?	£35.50
12	Ten percent of a number is sixteen. What is the number?	160
13	Write eight hundredths as a decimal.	0.08
14	What is seven tenths of forty?	28
15	When 132 is added to a number the answer is 474. What is the number?	342
	Fifteen Second Questions	
16	What is the median of these seven numbers: 26, 21, 17, 42, 16, 19 and 18?	19
17	If John saves 75p a week and needs £7.99 for a CD, how many weeks will it take?	11 weeks
18	What year is three hundred years after two thousand and six?	2306
19	Look at the graph on your sheet. How far will I have walked in 25 minutes?	2.5 km
20	Look at the table on your sheet. How many dinners are served in one week?	36 dinners

Book 4 Test 22 Pupil Answer Sheet

Name_____   Date_____   Total Score

Five Second Questions

1.
2. _____ children
3.
4.
5.
6.
7.
8.

Ten Second Questions

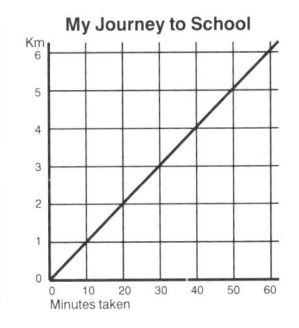

9.
10. five pence coins   5p , £15
11. £
12.
13.
14.
15. 132 , 474

Fifteen Second Questions

16. 26, 21, 17, 42, 16, 19, 18
17. _____ weeks   75p , £7.99
18.
19. _____ km

My Journey to School (graph, Km vs Minutes taken, 0–60)

20. _____ dinners

Children Having School Dinners	
Monday	4
Tuesday	6
Wednesday	0
Thursday	7
Friday	19

© Topical Resources. May be photocopied for classroom use only.

Book 4 Test 23 Teacher Questions

No.	Question	Answer
	Five Second Questions	
1	What is the nearest ten to ninety six?	100
2	How many five pence stamps can you buy with twenty pence?	4 x 5p stamps
3	What is seventy take away fifty?	20
4	Add together seven, five and sixteen.	28
5	Fourteen people share twenty eight sweets. How many do they get each?	2 sweets
6	What is four thousand six hundred divided by a thousand?	4.6
7	Change one hundred centimetres into millimetres.	1000 mm
8	In a survey 75% of people asked liked cycling. What fraction liked cycling?	$3/4$
	Ten Second Questions	
9	What is minus three added to eighteen?	15
10	If cuddly toys cost £7.99 each, how much will six cuddly toys cost?	£47.94
11	Multiply four by four and then subtract ten.	6
12	How many minutes are there in six and a half hours?	390 minutes
13	What is the size of this angle.	75° - 85°
14	What number is forty seven less than one hundred and six?	59
15	What is nine twenty-sevenths in its simplest form?	$1/3$
	Fifteen Second Questions	
16	What is the product of fifteen and twenty five?	375
17	What is the mean of: 10, 11, 13, 12 and 9 ?	11
18	If each square is 1 cm sq, what is the area of the shape to the nearest 1/2 cm sq.	$4^{1/2}$ cm^2 - $5^{1/2}$ cm^2
19	If a swimming pool is 30m by 22m what is its surface area?	660 m^2
20	What are the coordinates of the point marked on your sheet?	(-5, -4)

Book 4 Test 23 Pupil Answer Sheet

Name_____ Date_____ Total Score ☐

Five Second Questions

1. _____

2. _____ five pence stamps

3. _____

4. _____

5. _____ sweets

6. _____

7. _____ mm

8. _____

Ten Second Questions

9. _____ -3 , 18

10. £ _____ £7.99 , 6

11. _____

12. _____ minutes

13. _____ degrees

14. _____ 47 , 106

15. _____ 9/27

Fifteen Second Questions

16. _____ 15 , 25

17. _____ 10, 11, 13, 12, 9

18. _____ cm²

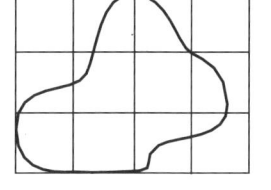

19. _____ m² 30m , 22m

20. _____

49

Book 4 Test 24 Teacher Questions

No.	Question	Answer
	Five Second Questions	
1	There are 102 children in a school. 50 are boys. How many are girls?	52 girls
2	What is half of forty?	20
3	What is the total of nine hundred, one and sixty?	961
4	What is eight multiplied by seven?	56
5	Subtract sixteen from sixty.	44
6	Write an even number more than 204 and less than 207.	206
7	What is ten percent of seventy?	7
8	Write the number that is twenty four less than three hundred.	276
	Ten Second Questions	
9	Seventy five percent of a number is twelve. What is the number?	16
10	What is fifteen percent of fifty?	7.5
11	One quarter of a number is thirty. What is the number?	120
12	What is the number shown by the arrow on your answer sheet.	20.54
13	What is half of five point two?	2.6
14	What is the size of this angle.	155° - 165°
15	Emily paid for a watch with a £50 note. She was given £5 change. How much was the watch?	£45
	Fifteen Second Questions	
16	What is the number exactly half way between 17.4 and 17.7?	17.55
17	What year is four hundred years after two thousand and three?	2403
18	Circle the middle number.	6.46
19	Circle two numbers which are multiples of seven.	21 & 14
20	Subtract the sum of 19 and 15 from 107.	73

Book 4 Test 24 Pupil Answer Sheet

Name_____ Date_____ Total Score ☐

Five Second Questions

1. _____ girls
2. _____
3. _____
4. _____
5. _____
6. _____
7. _____
8. _____

Ten Second Questions

9. _____
10. _____ 15% , 50

11. _____
12. _____ 20.5 ↓ 20.6
13. _____ 5.2
14. _____ degrees
15. _____ £

Fifteen Second Questions

16. _____ 17.4 , 17.7
17. _____
18. _____ 6.123, 6.46, 6.7
19. _____ 16 21 14 18 19 17
20. _____ 19 , 15 , 107

© Topical Resources. May be photocopied for classroom use only.

51

Book 4 Test 25 Teacher Questions

No.	Question	Answer
	Five Second Questions	
1	What is ten more than sixty four?	74
2	What is the total of twelve and thirteen?	25
3	What is the nearest ten to eighty seven?	90
4	How many thirties make ninety?	3
5	What is six hundred and seventy two divided by one hundred?	6.72
6	Write the number eight hundred and twelve thousand two hundred and six in figures.	812,206
7	Six people share twelve pounds equally. How much do they get each?	£2
8	What is forty eight divided by six?	8
	Ten Second Questions	
9	What number is fifty three less than one hundred and seventeen?	64
10	Ten percent of a number is two hundred. What is the number?	2000
11	Divide fifty six by eight and then add eleven.	18
12	The temperature in Lisbon is 13°C. In London it is -1°C. What is the difference?	14°C
13	A TV programme starts at 5 to 8. It lasts for 30 minutes. When does it finish?	8:25
14	Divide nine hundred by thirty.	30
15	Circle the two numbers that total ninety six.	27 & 69
	Fifteen Second Questions	
16	What is the mode of these six numbers: 26, 41, 28, 27, 26 and 42 ?	26
17	What is the number exactly half way between the two numbers on your sheet?	116
18	In a game there are six green balls and twenty red balls. What is the chance of picking a green ball?	6/26 or 3/13
19	Subtract the sum of sixteen and seventeen from one hundred and seven.	74
20	Circle the two numbers which are factors of fifty six.	7 & 8

Book 4 Test 25 Pupil Answer Sheet

Name_____   Date_____   Total Score ☐

Five Second Questions

1.
2.
3.
4.
5.
6.
7. £
8.

11.
12. °C   Lisbon 13°C
         London -1°C
13.   5 to 8 , 30 mins
14.
15.   27 , 12 , 69 , 80 , 70

Fifteen Second Questions

16.   26, 41, 28, 27, 26, 42
17.   109 , 123
18.   6 green balls
       20 red balls

Ten Second Questions

9.   53 , 117
10.

19.   16 , 17 , 107
20.   6 , 7 , 9 , 5 , 10 , 8

© Topical Resources. May be photocopied for classroom use only.

Book 4 Test 26 Teacher Questions

No.	Question	Answer
	Five Second Questions	
1	How many twenty five pence stamps can you buy with fifty pence?	2 stamps
2	What is ninety take away forty?	50
3	Write the next odd number after fifty nine.	61
4	Add together six, nine and twenty four.	39
5	What is double twenty six?	52
6	What is the square root of eighty one?	9
7	What is nine hundred and forty six to the nearest hundred?	900
8	What is one tenth of seventy?	7
	Ten Second Questions	
9	A magazine costs £2.49. How many can I buy with fifteen pounds?	6 magazines
10	Write three tenths as a decimal.	0.3
11	What is seven eighths of thirty two?	28
12	Multiply fourteen by ten and then add four.	144
13	A shop has a half price sale. A coat cost £101. How much is it now?	£50.50
14	What is minus seventeen added to twenty?	3
15	When 172 is added to a number the answer is 793. What is the number?	621
	Fifteen Second Questions	
16	Look at the pie chart. What is the fraction of children who prefer P.E.	3/8
17	Fiona saves 75p a week. She needs £8.99 to buy a CD. How long must she save?	12 weeks
18	What is the median of these seven numbers: 18, 19, 21, 42, 11, 12 and 14 ?	18
19	If a swimming pool measures 30m by 15m, what is its surface area?	450 m^2
20	Look at the table on your sheet. How many dinners are served in one week?	41 dinners

Book 4 Test 26 Pupil Answer Sheet

Name_____   Date_____   Total Score ☐

Five Second Questions

1	twenty five pence stamps
2	
3	
4	
5	
6	
7	
8	

Ten Second Questions

| 9 | magazines   £2.49 , £15 |
| 10 | |

11	
12	
13	£
14	−17 , 20
15	172 , 793

Fifteen Second Questions

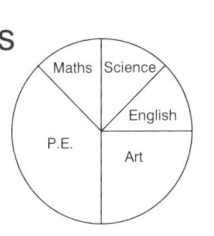

| 16 | |

Pie chart: Maths, Science, English, Art, P.E.

17	weeks 75p , £8.99
18	18, 19, 21, 42, 11, 12, 14
19	m² 30m , 15m
20	dinners

Children Having School Dinners

Monday	7
Tuesday	7
Wednesday	7
Thursday	6
Friday	14

© Topical Resources. May be photocopied for classroom use only.

Book 4 Test 27 Teacher Questions

No.	Question	Answer
	Five Second Questions	
1	There are thirty children in a class. Twelve are boys. How many are girls?	18 girls
2	What is the nearest ten to sixteen?	20
3	What is the total of nine, six hundred and seventy?	679
4	Eighteen people share thirty six sweets. How many do they get each?	2 sweets
5	Change two hundred and thirty centimetres into millimetres.	2300 mm
6	What is two point nine times one hundred?	290
7	In a survey 100% of the people liked to watch the news. What fraction liked to watch the news?	one whole
8	What is four squared?	16
	Ten Second Questions	
9	Picture frames cost £6.99 each. How much will seven picture frames cost?	£48.93
10	What is fifteen percent of thirty?	4.5
11	One quarter of a number is one hundred. What is the number?	400
12	What is the size of this angle.	345° - 355°
13	What is half of nineteen?	9.5
14	Ten percent of a number is three hundred. What is the number?	3000
15	A pen costs £3.50. How many pens can you buy with fifteen pounds?	4 pens
	Fifteen Second Questions	
16	What year is two hundred years after two thousand and two?	2202
17	What is the mean of 21, 29, 40 and 10?	25
18	In a game there are seven yellow and four blue balls. What is the chance of picking a blue ball?	4/11
19	What number is exactly half way between 6.2 and 6.5?	6.35
20	Michelle saves £1.25 a week. She needs £15 for a watch. How many weeks will it be before she can buy it?	12 weeks

Book 4 Test 27 Pupil Answer Sheet

Name_____   Date_____   Total Score

Five Second Questions

1	girls
2	
3	
4	sweets
5	mm
6	
7	
8	

Ten Second Questions

| 9 | £ | £6.99 , 7 |
| 10 | | 15% , 30 |

11	
12	degrees
13		19
14	
15	pens	£3.50 , £15

Fifteen Second Questions

16	
17		21, 29, 40, 10
18		7 yellow balls / 4 blue balls
19		6.2 , 6.5
20	weeks	£1.25 , £15

© Topical Resources. May be photocopied for classroom use only.

Book 4 Test 28 Teacher Questions

No.	Question	Answer
	Five Second Questions	
1	How many twenty pence stamps can you buy with sixty pence?	3 x 20p stamps
2	What is the total of twenty and thirty?	50
3	What is ten more than forty two?	52
4	Subtract thirty nine from eighty.	41
5	Write the number that is thirty two less than three hundred.	268
6	What is ten percent of seventy six?	7.6
7	What is eight multiplied by six?	48
8	Write an odd number more than 115 and less than 120.	117 or 119
	Ten Second Questions	
9	A TV programme starts at 10 to 6. It lasts for 36 minutes. When does it finish?	6:26
10	Ben paid for trainers with a £50 note. He had £2 and one penny in change. How much were they?	£47.99
11	What is minus seven added to eight?	1
12	Divide seven hundred and twenty by eighty.	9
13	What is the number shown by the arrow on your sheet.	100.04
14	CD's cost £8.99 each. How many CD's can I buy for £40 ?	4 CD's
15	Multiply seven hundred by two hundred.	140,000
	Fifteen Second Questions	
16	Subtract the sum of nineteen and eighteen from eighty six.	49
17	What is the number exactly half way between 126 and 148?	137
18	Circle the two numbers which are multiples of six.	42 & 12
19	Put these numbers in order, largest first. 9.632 , 9.9 , 9.12	9.9, 9.632, 9.12
20	Circle the two numbers which are factors of twenty eight.	4 & 7

Book 4 Test 28 Pupil Answer Sheet

Name_____ Date_____ Total Score

Five Second Questions

1. twenty pence stamps
2.
3.
4.
5.
6.
7.
8.

Ten Second Questions

9. 10 to 6 , 36 mins
10. £   £50 , £2.01

11. -7 , 8
12. 720 , 80
13.   100   100.1
14. CDs £8.99 , £40
15. 700 , 200

Fifteen Second Questions

16. 19 , 18 , 86
17. 126 , 148
18. 26 63 42 22 14 12
19. 9.632, 9.9, 9.12
20. 4 3 5 10 6 7

© Topical Resources. May be photocopied for classroom use only.

Book 4 Test 29 Teacher Questions

No.	Question	Answer
	Five Second Questions	
1	Write the next odd number after sixty three.	65
2	What is seventy take away sixty?	10
3	There are 29 children in a class. Two are absent. How many are present?	27 children
4	What is double forty six?	92
5	What is the square root of forty nine?	7
6	What is nought point six multiplied by ten?	6
7	Eight people share twenty four pounds equally. How much do they get each?	£3
8	What is twenty eight divided by seven?	4
	Ten Second Questions	
9	A shop has a half price sale. A dress was £125. How much does it cost now?	£62.50
10	One eighth of a number is seven. What is the number?	56
11	Circle the two numbers that total twenty four.	19 & 5
12	A TV programme starts at 10 to 10. It lasts for 25 minutes. When does it finish?	10:15
13	Multiply seventeen by ten and then add twenty.	190
14	Divide one hundred by ten and then add twenty eight.	38
15	A bag of potatoes costs £1.50. How many bags can I buy with £10?	6 bags
	Fifteen Second Questions	
16	What is the mode of these six numbers: 17, 27, 41, 41, 26 and 18.	41
17	Circle two numbers which are multiples of nine.	90 & 45
18	If Stewart saves £1.25 a week and he needs £11.99 to buy a shirt, how many weeks does he need to save for?	10 weeks
19	What number is exactly half way between 14.6 and 14.9?	14.75
20	Look at the table on your sheet. How many dinners are served in a week?	41 dinners

Book 4 Test 29 Pupil Answer Sheet

Name_____ Date_____ Total Score ☐

Five Second Questions

1. ☐
2. ☐
3. ☐ children
4. ☐
5. ☐
6. ☐
7. £ ☐
8. ☐

Ten Second Questions

9. £ ☐
10. ☐

11. ☐ 19 6 5 3 16
12. ☐ 10 to 10 , 25 mins
13. ☐
14. ☐
15. ☐ bags £1.50 , £10

Fifteen Second Questions

16. ☐ 17, 27, 41, 41, 26, 18
17. ☐ 90 41 26 37 45 17
18. ☐ weeks £1.25 , £11.99
19. ☐ 14.6 , 14.9
20. ☐ dinners

Children Having School Dinners	
Monday	8
Tuesday	8
Wednesday	6
Thursday	2
Friday	17

© Topical Resources. May be photocopied for classroom use only.

Book 4 Test 30 Teacher Questions

No.	Question	Answer
	Five Second Questions	
1	How many five pence stamps can you buy with fifteen pence?	3 x 5p stamps
2	What is ten subtracted from forty two?	32
3	What is the total of seven hundred, six and forty?	746
4	What is one hundred and twenty nine to the nearest ten?	130
5	How many fifteen's make forty five?	3
6	Change four point three metres into centimetres.	430cm
7	What is double thirty six?	72
8	What are two tenths of fifty?	10
	Ten Second Questions	
9	Multiply eight hundred by six hundred.	480,000
10	What is fifteen percent of three hundred?	45
11	What is nine hundredths of 400?	36
12	Write seven tenths as a decimal.	0.7
13	163 is added to a number. The answer is 999. What is the number?	836
14	One sixth of a number is eight. What is the number?	48
15	Circle the two numbers that total ninety three.	46 and 47
	Fifteen Second Questions	
16	What is the mean of one hundred, two hundred and six hundred?	300
17	What is the mode of these six numbers: 26, 26, 71, 42, 21 and 20 ?	26
18	In a game there are 9 red balls and 7 green balls. What is the chance of picking a green ball?	7/16
19	What is the median of these seven numbers: 14, 6, 27, 17, 19, 82 and 16?	17
20	Put these numbers in order, smallest first. 16.6, 16.061 and 16.25	16.061, 16.25, 16.6

Book 4 Test 30 Pupil Answer Sheet

Name_____ Date_____ Total Score [ ]

Five Second Questions

1. ____ five pence stamps
2. ____
3. ____
4. ____
5. ____
6. ____ cm
7. ____
8. ____

Ten Second Questions

9. ____   800 , 600
10. ____   15% , 300
11. ____
12. ____
13. ____   163 , 999
14. ____
15. ____   46 20 17 11 47

Fifteen Second Questions

16. ____   100 , 200 , 600
17. ____   26, 26, 71, 42, 21, 20
18. ____   9 red balls
         7 green balls
19. ____   14, 6, 27, 17, 19, 82, 16
20. ____   16.6, 16.061, 16.25

© Topical Resources. May be photocopied for classroom use only.

Pupil Record Sheet

Name_____

Colour in the boxes up to the correct score for each test.

	1	2	3	4	5	6	7	8	9	10	11	12	13	14	15	16	17	18	19	20
Test 1																				
Test 2																				
Test 3																				
Test 4																				
Test 5																				
Test 6																				
Test 7																				
Test 8																				
Test 9																				
Test 10																				
Test 11																				
Test 12																				
Test 13																				
Test 14																				
Test 15																				
Test 16																				
Test 17																				
Test 18																				
Test 19																				
Test 20																				
Test 21																				
Test 22																				
Test 23																				
Test 24																				
Test 25																				
Test 26																				
Test 27																				
Test 28																				
Test 29																				
Test 30	1	2	3	4	5	6	7	8	9	10	11	12	13	14	15	16	17	18	19	20

© **Topical Resources.** May be photocopied for classroom use only.